D0762302

DISCARD

Everything You Need to Know About

A DRUG-ABUSING PARENT

A drug-abusing parent causes many problems in a family.

• THE NEED TO KNOW LIBRARY •

Everything You Need to Know About
A DRUG-ABUSING PARENT

Frances Shuker-Haines

THE ROSEN PUBLISHING GROUP, INC.
NEW YORK

Published in 1994 by The Rosen Publishing Group, Inc.
29 East 21st Street, New York, NY 10010

First Edition
Copyright 1994 by The Rosen Publishing Group, Inc.

Manufactured in the United States of America.

Library of Congress Cataloging-in-Publication Data

Shuker-Haines, Frances.
    Everything you need to know about a drug abusing parent /
Frances Shuker-Haines.—1st ed.
        p. cm.
    Includes bibliographical references and index.
ISBN 0-8239-1529-8
    1.Children of narcotic addicts—United States—Family relation-
ships—Juvenile literature. 2. Narcotic addicts—United States—Family
relationships—Juvenile literature. [1. Drug abuse. 2. Parent and child.]
I. Title.
HV5824.C45S54   1993
362.29'13—dc20   93-32182
                                                                      CIP
                                                                       AC

Contents

Introduction

This is a book for kids whose parents take drugs or drink too much. It is for kids whose parents are "substance abusers." The substance can be cocaine, marijuana, crack, tranquilizers, painkillers, heroin, alcohol, or any other drug. You may be surprised that alcohol is in this list. But alcohol is a drug, and it is often abused. When this book refers to the children of drug abusers—it includes the children of alcoholics.

Chances are, if you are the child of a substance abuser, you already know it. You know when your parent's drug or drinking habit is causing trouble in your family. But you might need to know more

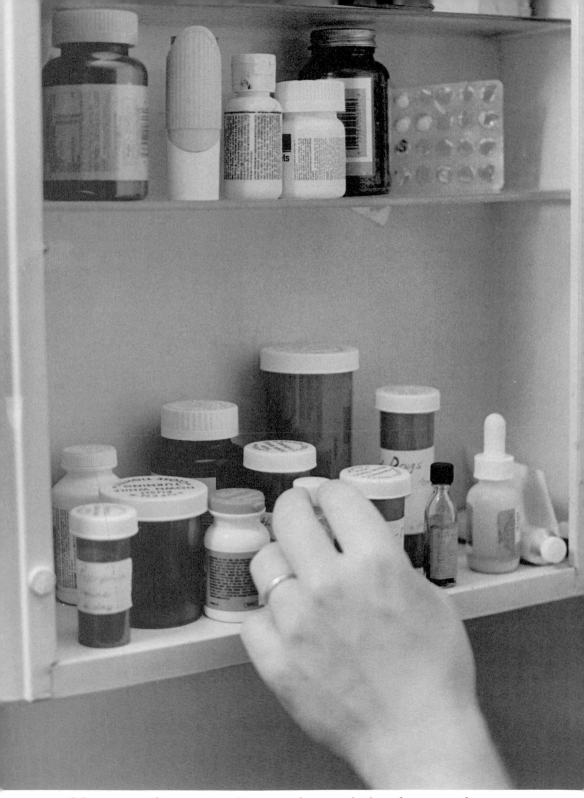

Many over-the-counter drugs and prescription drugs can become addictive.

about your parent's problem and what you can and can't do to help. You might need to know more about what is happening to you and the *millions* of other kids like you.

As a child of a drug-abusing parent, it is important to remember these things:

You are not alone. Many other people are going through exactly what you are going through. Many people have already been through this and survived. There are lots of people who can and will help you. This book will show you how to get the support you need. It will help you care for the most important person affected by your parent's drug use: you.

Your parent is suffering from a disease. Your mother or father is not a substance abuser because she or he is a bad person. Your parent is sick, just as someone with cancer is sick. Your mother or father needs help. The difference is that your mother or father may not believe that he or she needs help. This *denial* is one of the symptoms of your parent's disease.

Your parent's drug problem is not your fault. You did not cause your parent's drug problem. Nothing that you did or do has made your parent into a substance abuser. Nothing you do now will make the abuse stop. No matter what anyone may say, no matter what you may think, this is not your fault in any way. Your parents are responsible for their own behavior. Not you.

You can live a drug-free life. Even though children of drug-abusing parents are at increased risk, you can take steps now to protect yourself. You can understand and care about your parent's problem, while keeping your self-esteem in good shape.

Reading this book is a great first step. It means you are no longer pretending that everything is okay. You are saying to yourself and the world that there is a problem and you want to do something about it. It means that you want to help yourself. Those are all great things to be thinking and feeling. You *are* important. You deserve help.

A person addicted to drugs has a constant need to satisfy the addiction.

Chapter 1

What Is Drug Abuse?

First, let's discuss what drugs really are. Drugs are any kind of substance—a pill, a drink, a cigarette—that makes your mind, your mood, or your body feel or act differently than it normally would. Some drugs are good—they can make sick people well, or ease the pain of people who are badly hurt. You've probably taken drugs like aspirin, cough or cold medicine, penicillin or other antibiotics. All of these drugs are legal, and they are sometimes necessary for medical reasons.

But sometimes people take legal drugs for non-medical reasons. They may become "hooked" on a drug they were given by a doctor. They may use the drug in a larger amount or for a longer time than they should. This is abuse. With alcohol, for example, it is considered abuse if used by kids under the legal drinking age (usually 21) or by adults who use it to excess.

Some people use drugs that are illegal. These drugs include cocaine, crack, marijuana, heroin, LSD, amphetamines (uppers), barbiturates (downers), and many others. These drugs harm the body and change behavior. These drugs are called abused drugs.

Some people are able to use drugs and alcohol without becoming abusers. But many people cannot. Some drugs are very *addictive*, and people can develop a physical or mental need for the drugs after using them only a few times. Drug abuse can mean many things. Here are some of the ways you can tell if someone has a drug/alcohol problem.

A drug abuser:

- cannot stop using or drinking
- turns into a "different" person when she or he is using the drug
- makes excuses for using drugs ("I had a bad day at the office . . .")
- tries to cover up his or her drug use, or pretend it "isn't that bad"
- forgets things that happen while she or he is on drugs or drunk
- won't admit that she or he has a problem.

Not every substance abuser does all of these things, but most of them do at least one or two of these things. An easy way to know if your parent is a drug abuser is to trust your instincts. If you feel that his or her use of drugs is a problem, then it is. Kids shouldn't have to worry that their parents are doing something unhealthy or illegal. If your parent's use of drugs makes you uneasy, scared, or angry, then your parent is abusing drugs and needs to stop.

How Did This Happen?

You might wonder how your parent became a substance abuser. That's not easy to answer. The reasons are different for each person. Here are a few reasons why your parent *may* have become a substance abuser:

Some drugs are very addictive. Your parent might have tried crack or heroin a few times to be sociable or out of curiosity. He or she may have enjoyed the way the drug made him or her feel. Without meaning to, your parent may have become addicted. Now your parent's body "needs" the drug to avoid having painful and often frightening physical symptoms.

Substance abuse tends to run in families. Your parent may have had a parent who was also a substance abuser. Children of substance abusers are much more likely to become substance abusers than other children.

Tragedy. Sometimes bad things happen in life. Some people turn to drugs or alcohol to help them get through a hard time. They may take drugs to help numb the pain. They may take drugs to keep feeling "up" when life is getting them down. The problem is that drugs can't solve problems. They can only make more problems.

An accident, a disease, or a physical ailment. Some people become addicted to prescription drugs. These are drugs that are given to people by doctors to help them get well or feel better when they are sick. What starts out as a help gets out of control and turns into abuse.

Try to remember that no one *means* to become a drug addict or an alcoholic. Your parent is sick. He or she deserves a chance to get help. Everyone deserves a drug-free life—your parent and you.

Chapter 2

The Effects of Drug Abuse on Your Parent

Y ou may already know that substance abuse is doing something to your mother or father that is scary and dangerous. You are right. It is called substance "abuse" for a reason: The substance is not being used right or well. It is hurting the person who takes it.

Changes in Mind and Body

Jennifer knew her father was changing, but she didn't know why. She could see that he was losing weight and seemed to be nervous all the time. He was coming home late from work quite often, too. Jennifer helped her mom make dinner. They would save a plate for her father, but he was never hungry.

"I ate at the office," he would say. Jennifer didn't believe him—he wouldn't be getting so skinny if he wasn't skipping meals.

When her father was home, he chain-smoked at the table and laughed loudly at silly things. He didn't pay attention to what Jennifer had to say; he just kept talking, not really making any sense.

One day, her father came home even later than usual and it worried Jennifer. He seemed wild and all wound up. He'd be laughing and talking fast one minute, then yelling the next. Jennifer didn't know what to expect. For the first time in her life she was frightened of her own father.

He could barely wake up the next morning and he was in a terrible mood all day. Jennifer was upset, too. "What's wrong with Daddy?" she finally asked her mother. "He's so different than he used to be." Her mother sat down and explained to Jennifer that her Dad had a serious problem—a drug problem. He was addicted to cocaine.

Some of the bad things that drugs do to your parent are physical. Drugs known as "uppers" or stimulants (like cocaine and crack) can make a person's heart race and, in some cases, cause a heart attack. Uppers may also cause people to become jumpy, fidgety, nervous, confused, and aggressive. And when the drug's effect wears off, the user may become depressed, tired, and unable to care for himself or herself.

Addiction to nicotine from cigarettes may lead to other drug abuse.

Drugs known as "downers" or sedatives (like Valium or alcohol) slow down the central nervous system and make people feel sleepy and slow. Downers make people unable to react quickly or to do things that require a lot of coordination, like driving a car. They usually make it difficult to think clearly. And often downers cause people to feel depressed. Narcotics (like heroin or morphine), which are very strong painkillers, many times have the same effects.

Drugs known as hallucinogens (like marijuana or LSD) cause people to see and hear things that aren't there. People feel as if they are dreaming even when they are awake. They often don't know what is real.

Any drug can harm your parent if it is used incorrectly. Substance abuse can damage the heart, the liver, or the brain. An abuser can also die from overdoses of drugs or alcohol.

Substance abusers can also hurt themselves and others through accidents or risky behavior. Drugs can cause someone to fall down, to walk across a busy street against the light, to drive a car recklessly, or to take unnecessary chances.

Changes in Behavior

You have seen that drugs can change your parent's mood, mind, and body. *Being* a drug abuser may also cause your parent to behave in strange, yet somewhat predictable, ways.

Drug use may cause a parent's behavior to change suddenly. This creates confusion and anguish for other family members.

Mark's mom likes to give parties. She is always inviting people over. She and her friends mix all kinds of drinks. Mark's mom gets really silly and sloppy when she drinks. Mark hates to see her like that—it's so embarrassing.

Over and over Mark or his dad suggests daytime activities that don't involve drinking. But Mom wants no part of them. She says it won't be any fun. It seems like Mom is always looking for an opportunity to drink. "Let's celebrate the first day of Spring!" she'll say, and fix herself a drink. Or, "Look at Mark's great report card; he deserves a toast."

One day, Mark's family decides to go on a picnic. They had not been out together as a family for a long time. Mark and his dad pack a cooler with sandwiches, chips, fruit, and soft drinks. But as soon as they spread the blanket, Mark's mother starts searching for a beer or a bottle of wine.

Mark's dad tells her that she doesn't need an alcoholic drink. He says she drinks too much and should "give it a rest." She looks at him blankly. "I don't know what you're talking about," she says. "I'm not some wino lying in the gutter somewhere. I just want to have a little fun. What's wrong with that?"

The next thing they know, she heads for the car and is off to find "a little something." Mark and his dad know she is going to get a drink. The picnic is ruined. Sometimes Mark feels that drinking is all his mother cares about. It is more important than a picnic. It is more important than anything.

Family relationships often suffer as a result of drug abuse.

Putting the drug use before anything else. The drug becomes all-important. Your mom or dad is addicted to the drug—dependent on it—and cannot control the use of it. Even if your parent loves you, he or she may take advantage of you or put you in danger to get more drugs. If your drug-abusing parent does not get help, the drug will take over his or her life.

Blaming everyone else. This is typical of the "disease" of substance abuse. The abuser needs excuses to use drugs. So the abuser accuses others of making him or her drink or do drugs. "You're driving me to drink!" "You kids make me so crazy, I need to take a pill to calm down!" "I'd be okay, if my boss gave me a chance."

Pretending that the drug problem isn't a problem. A substance abuser often pretends to "forget" the embarrassing and harmful things that happen while he or she is "high" on drugs or drunk. Sometimes the abuser is so drunk or "wasted" that he or she really can't remember what happened. Your mom or dad may not believe what you say because he or she is too ashamed and afraid to face the problem.

Changes in Parenting

Substance abuse also hurts people's parenting. A parent who puts drugs first is not considering the needs of his or her kids. A parent who is "stoned" or drunk can't make good decisions or handle

A drug-abusing parent often blames other people or events for his or her addiction.

emergencies. A parent who gets loud or argumen-
tative or depressed while using drugs can be scary
and dangerous. A parent who causes family problems and will not admit it is not a good role model.
A parent who loses a job because of his or her drug
abuse is not providing for the family.

Do any of these sentences describe one of your
parents? You may be very angry about the ways in
which your mother or father is not a good parent.
You have every right to be. All children deserve
loving parents who nurture and care for them.

Why Substance Abuse Is a "Disease"

In this book we often refer to substance abuse
as a disease. Doctors and substance-abuse experts
describe it as a disease for many reasons. These
are some of the reasons:

1. It follows a pattern that is the same for most
   people.
2. It has symptoms that are the same for most
   people.
3. It gets worse if it is not treated.
4. There is a standard (generally accepted) way
   to treat it.

Before doctors started calling substance abuse a
disease, people thought that abusers were just
"weak" or "bad." People believed that if abusers
tried harder and really wanted to change, they
could stop abusing drugs. Now we know that the
abusers are not bad; they are just powerless to

control what is happening. They need trained people to help them learn about their disease and how to stay away from drugs forever. One way drug addiction and alcoholism are different from some diseases is that a person can get better, but he or she can never be completely cured. Drug abusers are *in recovery* for the rest of their lives. They will never be able to use any amount of the drug again without risking a relapse of the disease.

Thinking about your parent's drug problem as a disease may help you, too. It may help you stop blaming yourself. After all, you couldn't give your parents cancer, could you? Well, you can't "give them" drug addiction either. Your drug-abusing parent is truly sick, but your taking the blame for his or her problem only makes recovery more difficult.

The truth is that your mother or father never meant to be a bad parent. You may find it hard to believe, but your mother or father wants only the best for you. This terrible disease of drug abuse prevents him or her from giving you the best. The good parent your mother or father means to be is still "in there" somewhere. And, someday, if your mother or father gets help, you may see that parent again.

Children of substance abusers usually feel confused and disturbed about their life at home.

Chapter 3

The Effects of a Parent's Drug Abuse on You

*J*ulie remembers the feeling of coming home and trying to prepare herself for her father's condition. Before she even walked in the door, she would wonder if he would be high. Would he try to corner her and talk about stuff that he wouldn't remember tomorrow? Would he and her mother be arguing? Julie was always scared to bring friends over, because she didn't want them to see her father drunk or find him passed out on the kitchen table. Sometimes at night, Julie and her sister would huddle together in the bathroom, waiting for the fighting to stop. Sometimes the girls would be very quiet, listening for their father's heavy footsteps to pass by their room, hoping he wouldn't come and bother them. All they wanted was for him to be a normal dad.

Having a parent who is a substance abuser is very hard. It can make kids feel sad, angry, confused, depressed, and afraid. The main thing for you to remember is that any way you feel about your parent's drug abuse is okay. Except for one thing—feeling guilty. Many children of substance abusers feel that they are the cause of their parent's addiction. They think that if they were better-behaved children, worked harder in school, were more helpful around the house, or worked part-time, maybe then their parent would stop abusing drugs. But that isn't true. You are *not* the reason your parent abuses drugs. And you can't make him or her stop abusing drugs. Only your parent can do that—with the right kind of help.

Trying to Cope

Being mad and upset day after day is a hard way to live. Not knowing what to expect from a drug-abusing parent can be very stressful. Different kids deal with their feelings in different ways. Some children of substance abusers become very quiet and withdrawn. They may have "learned" to be this way at home to keep a drunk or drugged parent from getting mad. Or they may try to keep their own anger hidden inside because they are afraid to explode and lose control.

Other kids living with a drug-abusing parent become loud and rowdy. They may become the "class clowns," or "wise guys" who make up stories to shock friends. They may be trying to "let out" some of their anger in ways that don't seem so bad.

Some kids create problems for themselves and others. They skip school or break rules. They do things that are mean or harmful. These kids may be so angry they just can't control themselves. Or so depressed they don't care what happens to them. Since they feel ignored at home, they try to get attention any way they can.

A drug-abusing parent in the house can make some kids take on too much responsibility. Some kids look after their younger brothers and sisters day and night. They cook the meals, do the grocery shopping, do the laundry, and may have to pay the bills. They may even be the ones to clean up after Mom or Dad when the parent has been on a binge. These overworked kids try to create some order in their lives. They try to have the "normal" life their parents can't give them. But they are paying a high price—their childhood.

Problem with Self-Esteem

Most kids who grow up with a substance-abusing parent also suffer from low *self-esteem*. That means they don't think they are very important. Children of substance abusers are often put down, criticized, or abused. They begin to think they don't deserve to have good things happen to them. They think that they must be bad kids, or else bad things wouldn't be happening to them.

Teens may be faced with greater responsibilities if they need to take over for a parent with a drug problem.

Of course, that isn't true. Kids whose parents
use drugs aren't bad kids. They shouldn't be made
to feel that they don't deserve good things. They
do. If you feel this way, you will have to keep re-
minding yourself that you are a good person in a
bad situation. You have to tell yourself that you are
not to blame for what is happening to you, your
parent, and your family.

Dealing with Abuse

Unfortunately, parents who are dependent on
drugs or alcohol are often abusive to their children.
They can't think clearly. The abuse may happen in
different ways; it could be mental or physical. But
it is always used to control another person. Some
people get angry and upset easily when they are
drunk or do drugs. Some people feel powerful.
Some just act mean. They hurt the people around
them. If this sometimes happens in your house,
you *must* figure out a safe place you can go. Parents are not allowed to hurt their children. You do
not *ever* deserve to be hurt.

Sexual abuse can be one of the most hurtful
types of abuse. Sexual abuse means using a child
for sexual pleasure. This is when someone touches
a child on his or her genitals (vagina or penis),
buttocks, or breasts. Or makes a child touch the
private parts of another person. Or forces a kid to
perform sexual acts. Any kind of touching that you
don't like is abuse. If sexual abuse is happening in

Finding a friend to confide in may help in coping with a bad family situation.

your house, find someone you can trust to talk to right away, even if your parent told you to keep it a "secret." Keep talking about the abuse until someone believes you. It is wrong for your parent (or anyone) to abuse you, and it should be stopped.

The Cycle Continues

One of the saddest things that can happen to the children of substance abusers is that they can also become substance abusers. In fact, if your parent abuses drugs or alcohol, you are *much* more likely to suffer from the same disease than people who grow up with parents who are not addicts. No one knows for sure how many kids will become addicts, but studies have shown that 40 to 60 percent of children with chemically dependent parents will become chemically dependent themselves. Every child in this situation is certainly at risk.

Is it "genetic"? That is, do these kids inherit the disease at birth, the way they inherit eye color or hair color or the shape of their ears? That is a question that is still not fully researched. Scientists have done studies, however, with adopted children who had birth parents who were substance abusers. A lot of those kids grew up to be substance abusers, even though the parents who raised them were not. That makes scientists think the disease of drug addiction may be somewhat genetic. But further studies need to be done in order to be sure.

It is likely that growing up in an unhappy home will make you an unhappy adult. And many unhappy adults turn to alcohol and drugs for "help." This is especially true when children have grown up watching their own parents turn to drugs to solve their problems or escape from them. That's why it is so important to get help for yourself now.

You must learn new ways to help yourself and new reasons to love yourself. And that's why you must understand that you are at risk. You, of all people, need to develop healthy ways to deal with stress, peer pressure, a broken home, or any of life's other problems that you may have to face.

Many children of substance abusers grow up thinking, "It will never happen to me!" They may think that because they have seen how horrible drug abuse is, they will not get hooked. They may feel safe enough even to experiment with drugs—"I know when to stop!" But it doesn't take long before these children lose control and become chemically dependent.

One of the painful things about drug abuse is "denial." Drug abusers convince themselves that they don't have a problem when it's obvious that they do. This is another reason to be careful. Once you become addicted, you are no longer reasonable. That is why avoiding drugs in the first place is the safest, surest way to stay drug-free.

Don't hurt yourself the way your parents are hurting themselves. Don't hurt others the way you are hurting now. You can break the cycle. You can keep yourself drug-free and enjoy your life.

Children of drug-abusing parents sometimes mistakenly think that getting rid of the substance will get rid of the problem.

Chapter 4

What You Can't Do

Kids who live with a drug-abusing parent often wish they could make their parent stop drinking or getting high. But kids can't "fix" their parent. Kids can't change their parent's habits. Kids can't cure their parent's disease.

You are not to blame, and there is nothing you can do to make your parent stop taking drugs. But your mother or father *can* get better. Your mom or dad *can* stop being a substance abuser. But *you* can't force your parent into recovery. The decision to stop drinking or stop using drugs is personal. Only when your mom or dad admits the problem and gets help will recovery begin.

Enabling and Codependency

Kids want their lives to be normal. They may
sometimes do almost anything to make it seem that
way. Sometimes they may "cover up" a parent's
drug use to protect their younger brothers and
sisters. They may say, for example, "Mom's just
having a bad day, it's nothing to worry about." Or,
"Dad was out late last night and needs his sleep
this morning." Sometimes they do work around
the house that is the parent's responsibility. Or,
they may make excuses for the drug-abusing parent when a promise is not kept. "It's okay, Mom,
that you missed my game today. It probably would
have given you a headache."

Kids who try to hide, "help," or make excuses
for their parent's drug abuse are called *enablers*.
Although they often mean well, pretending that
everything in their home is fine makes it easier for
(enables) the drug abuse to continue. When a
drug-abuser's spouse (husband or wife) is affected
by the chemical dependency of the other, he or she
is called *codependent*. Codependents also allow the
drug abuse in the home to continue. And they can
get so caught up in their spouse's disease that they
forget to take care of their own needs. As the drug
dependency gets worse, the codependency gets
worse. This disorder can become very serious,
even life-threatening.

It is not easy to stop the enabling. If your parent
is abusing drugs, you are probably trying your best

Many children of substance abusers cover up for their parent's problem by taking care of all the chores and trying to smooth out conflicts.

to get through each day. But it's time to let yourself "off the hook." Stop cleaning up after your
parent. Stop lying to protect him or her. Stop pretending that you aren't angry. Stop trying to be
perfect. Try to remember that nothing you do or
don't do will make your parent stop. The *only* thing
you can do for your parent is to let him or her suffer the consequences of the drug abuse. Drug
abusers need to see what their abuse is doing to
themselves and the people around them.

Chapter 5

What You Can Do

Okay, you can't fix it, you can't blame yourself, and you can't make it stop—the drug abuse is your parent's problem. But there are many things you can do to help yourself. And you deserve it.

Share the Secret

You are not a bad son or daughter if you talk about your parent's drug problem. What is going on inside your home may be very painful and upsetting for you. There is no need to go through this alone. If you can admit that there is a problem, you have taken an important first step. You will start to feel better when you begin talking honestly and openly about your feelings.

There are many people available who are ready to listen, and who can support you at this difficult time. When you decide that it's time to start taking care of yourself, you can get in touch with:

Your school guidance counselor or a teacher. These staff members are trained to help young people as they grow into adulthood. They may be working with other students who have a drug-abusing parent. Or they may be able to refer you to another professional who specializes in your kind of family problem.

Your priest, minister, or rabbi. It may be comforting to talk with someone who already knows your family. He or she will not tell anyone about your conversations but may be able to suggest other people you can contact.

A trusted relative or adult friend. A grown-up who knows you well and cares about you may be the easiest person to talk to. This person may offer the love, support, and encouragement that you have missed for a long time. He or she may also offer you a place to stay when you need to "get away" and think about things more clearly.

A friend. Millions of children are growing up in families like yours. Chances are, someone you know is going through the same thing you are. Talking to a friend can help, even if your friend's parents are not substance abusers. Friends are there to love you and let you know you're okay. A good friend wants only the best for you.

A teacher or counselor may be able to offer advice on where to get further help.

Learn More About It

Drug and alcohol abuse are complex problems. More and more is being written about their causes, their treatment, and how the whole family is affected. This book, and others mentioned in the back of this book, can explain some important things about substance abuse. The more you learn about addiction, the more you will understand your drug-abusing parent and what is happening to you. You can learn to separate yourself from your parent's problem and live your own life.

Protect Yourself and Get Help

You have a right to be safe. Anytime you feel that you are in serious danger in your home, leave immediately. Go to the house of a neighbor, friend, or relative. Or go to some other safe place. If you cannot leave, try at least to get to a phone. Call 911 and say that you have a police emergency.

Some kids are turning in their drug-abusing parent to the police even if they are not at risk. They know that many drugs are illegal and dangerous, and they want their parent to stop using. But this is a serious step for kids to take on their own. There are many things to consider. Although no one can tell you for sure whether this would be the right thing for you to do, an adult may be able to advise you.

Help is always available to young people who join *Alateen*. This nationwide organization brings

together the teenage children of substance abusers. They meet in groups to discuss their experi-
ences and their feelings. They give each other love
and support. They let each other know that they
don't have to feel "different" or alone anymore.
Al-Anon is a similar organization that helps to meet
the needs of the family of substance abusers.

Try to remember that helping yourself is also
about pleasing yourself—being good to you. Do
the kinds of things that make you happy. Work on
that self-esteem. Keep telling yourself positive
things about you. Hang out with people that believe in you. And start believing in yourself.

The understanding and caring of friends can be a great help for teens involved in a bad family situation.

Chapter 6

How to Help a Friend

Katie had always been best friends with Sarah. They grew up on the same block. They shared everything and spent a lot of time with each other. They often did their homework together, and they spoke on the phone every night.

But lately, Katie has noticed some changes in Sarah. Sometimes when Katie calls, Sarah says she can't talk and just hangs up without explaining. It seems that Sarah is alway in a hurry to get away from her friend. Katie is worried. She's certain that Sarah isn't doing all her homework—and that's not like Sarah either.

Sarah started making excuses why it was not convenient for Katie to come over to her house. Katie was beginning to wonder what was going on.

One day, Sarah began asking strange questions about Katie's father. Sarah wanted to know what he was "like" at home. She asked Katie if her father was ever mean. Did he ever hit her or make her feel uncomfortable in any way? Katie said no. She told her friend that her dad was a pretty nice guy. He had strict rules about schoolwork and TV, but he was kind. Sarah started to cry. Katie didn't know why.

The last time Sarah came over to spend the night at Katie's house, Katie's whole family had dinner together. Everybody was talking about their day and laughing. Again, Sarah started to cry. She ran from the table and Katie ran after her. "What's wrong, Sarah? Why are you so upset?" Katie asked. "I wish I had your family," said Sarah. "My family is just a big mess. I can't take it anymore." Then Sarah finally told her friend a family secret—Sarah's dad was an alcoholic.

Some of you reading this book may be worried about a friend. It's great to be concerned, because most kids whose parents are substance abusers need lots of understanding, support, and love. But what if your friend is too embarrassed to tell you that he or she has a serious family problem. How can you tell if something is wrong? There may be warning signs like the ones Katie noticed about Sarah. If you can answer yes to more than one of the following questions, your friend may be having trouble at home:

Avoiding a close friend may be a sign of a troubled teen.

- Has your friend stopped inviting you over? There may be a parent at home your friend doesn't want you to see. Or it might be because your friend wants to spend as much time as possible away from home.
- Does your friend make lots of excuses for his or her parent's behavior? Ask yourself how *your* parent would act in a similar situation.
- Does your friend seem depressed? Depressed people often sleep too much, or not sleep at all. They may lose interest in things they once enjoyed. And they may seem not to care about what happens to them. Depression that goes on for a long time may become serious. Listen closely to what your friend is saying. Take it seriously, especially if there is any talk of suicide. He or she may need professional help as well as a good friend.
- Has your friend started to do poorly in school? Sometimes things at home can get so bad that it is impossible for kids even to think about school.
- Has your friend started to drink or experiment with drugs?

If you think a friend is having trouble at home, ask him or her if there's something going on. Be honest. Tell your friend that you are concerned. Be specific about your reasons for being concerned. Your friend may not open up to you right away. He or she may still pretend that everything is fine. Keep trying. Let your friend know that you are always willing to listen.

Showing That You Care

Being a good listener is very important. It's easy to do. Just listen! Let your friend talk about the problem any way he or she wants to. Don't jump in with too many ideas or opinions. Let your friend tell you how he or she feels.

When your friend has finished talking, let him or her know that you care a lot about what is happening. Offer to help in any way you can.

You may want to invite your friend over to your house for a day or so (check with your parents first). You can try to help your friend think of a trusted adult to talk to. Or go with your friend to an Alateen meeting. Doing new things can be scary, even when they are good things to do.

The support of a friend can make a difference. But remember, you can't *solve* your friend's problems. And you can't give up everything in your own life for your friend. If you are trying to help a friend with this problem, let *your* mom or dad know what you are doing. Being a good friend can be hard work. Your parents will want to make sure that you are taking care of yourself, too.

Getting family counseling is the beginning of working out problems and reestablishing healthy relationships.

Chapter 7

Making Things Better

There is hope for the children of drug-abusing parents. It may be hard to believe, but things can get better! Lots and lots of substance abusers *do* get help. They stop doing drugs or drinking and go back to living normal lives. Someday it could happen to your mom or dad.

If it does happen, the whole family will have to change. Everyone will have to learn to relate to one another in healthy ways. You may all need to meet with a therapist or counselor to talk about your feelings. It may take a while to deal with the pain the disease of substance abuse has caused your family. You may be angry for a long time afterward. But you'll be surprised at how well families can heal if they work together.

53

Your parent may start attending "12-step" meetings, like Alcoholics Anonymous or Narcotics Anonymous. These meetings are very important. They help your mother or father learn why he or she became addicted to drugs and how to stay away from drugs. They can prepare your mother or father for a life without drugs. They also help your mother or father understand that she or he will always have the disease of substance abuse and can keep it under control only by never having alcohol or drugs again.

Many thousands of people have had a kind of "spiritual awakening" as a result of these steps, and have been able to live drug-free lives ever since.

It Takes More Than Love

No matter how much you and your parent love each other, it is also possible that your parent won't ever get the help she or he needs. Chemical dependency is a progressive, chronic disease; there is always the possibility of relapse. That will always be painful for you. But you must take charge of your own life. You have choices. You can make a better life for yourself even if your parent's life goes on as before. Your parent's disease does not have to destroy you. Set your own goals. Plan for your future by doing the best you can now.

Try making a list for yourself like the one on page 57. Include some positive statements about yourself and some important messages that you

Teens can help themselves by planning their lives and working toward goals that will bring self-esteem and satisfaction.

Focusing on their own talents and ambitions will enable the children
of substance abusers to survive and move forward in life.

want to become part of your thinking. Read over
the list every day.

1. I am a special person with my own attitudes
   and opinions.
2. I am in charge of my own life.
3. I make my own decisions and take responsibility for my own mistakes.
4. I will forgive myself when I make mistakes.
5. I will express myself honestly and openly.
6. I deserve to be treated with consideration
   and respect.
7. I will try to learn something from every
   experience I have in life (even the ones I
   don't like).

An Example to Remember

Bill Clinton's stepfather was an abusive alcoholic. Bill's brother was a drug addict. And yet,
Bill Clinton grew up to be a top scholar and to
attend the finest schools. He became Governor of
Arkansas and was elected President of the United
States in 1992. Keep him in mind as you make your
way through these difficult years. Bill did not
choose to remain a *victim*. He moved beyond self-
pity. He became a *survivor* instead. He believed in
his own ability—and he went ahead to accomplish
great things. So can you!

A Note from the Author

I am also the child of a substance abuser. My father was an alcoholic most of my childhood. He stopped drinking when I was 18 years old. I was often very sad while I was growing up. Sometimes I was scared. Sometimes I was mad. Sometimes I was very embarrassed. I never told anyone what was going on in my house. Once, when I was a grown-up, I found out that a friend of mine also had an alcoholic father. It was such a relief to talk to him! I found out that he had felt just the way I had, and that I was not alone! How I wished I could have talked to someone when I was younger and trying to cope.

I am living proof that you can survive this. I want you to survive this, too. Get all the help you can. Believe in yourself. Look forward to the rest of your life. And don't overlook the positive things in your life— good friends, ice cream, opening day of the baseball season. There is joy to be had, and you deserve it!

Glossary—*Explaining New Words*

chronic Lasting a long time or recurring.

codependent A person affected by someone else's chemical dependence.

drunk Condition that occurs when too much alcohol is taken into the body. Drunk people cannot think clearly or act normally.

enabler Someone who protects a substance abuser from the harmful effects of his or her addiction. Person who helps another to remain dependent on a drug.

"high" or "stoned" Describing someone who is on drugs.

narcotic Drug that is intended to ease pain.

progressive Continuing by successive steps.

recovery Healing time after a substance abuser stops using drugs.

relapse A falling back into a former condition after it seemed to be improved.

sedative Drug that is intended to relax people and make them sleepy.

self-esteem A person's feelings about himself or herself.

stimulant Drug that is intended to make people feel more alert and peppy.

substance abuser Someone who uses drugs and/or alcohol so much that it is causing problems for himself or herself and for others.

substance-abuse professional Person who has special education and experience in the disease of substance abuse and who is trained to help substance abusers get better.

symptom Physical sign of a medical problem.

tranquilizer Drug that is intended to relax people and make them less nervous or upset.

Where to Get Help

There are many organizations and people that you can call to get help:

A family member, guidance counselor, teacher, social worker, priest, minister, rabbi, or any other trusted adult.

Alateen is a group of teenagers just like you who meet to discuss their problems and ways of coping. There is no "800" number, so look in the white or yellow pages of your phone book for the number of your local group.

Al-Anon is a group for families of alcohol and drug abusers. Call 1-800-344-2666 for information.

The Drug and Alcohol Helpline: 1-800-662-4357
The Children of Alcoholics Foundation:
1-800-359-COAF   (1-800-359-2623)

There may be several clinics, hospitals, mental health facilities, or private treatment centers in your area that specialize in drug-abuse problems. Look in the phone book under "Drugs" or "Drug Abuse," "Alcohol" or "Alcoholism," "Counseling," "Social Workers," or "Psychologists."

For Further Reading

Alateen—Hope for Children of Alcoholics. New York: Al-Anon Family Group Headquarters, Inc., 1989.

Black, Claudia. *My Dad Loves Me, My Dad Has a Disease*. Denver: MAC Publishing, 1982.

Leite, Evelyn, and Espeland, Pamela. *Different Like Me: A Book for Teens Who Worry about Their Parents' Use of Alcohol/Drugs.* Minneapolis: Johnson Institute Books, 1987.

McFarland, Rhoda. *Drugs and Your Parents,* rev. ed. New York: The Rosen Publishing Group, 1993.

Seixas, Judith S. *Living with a Parent Who Drinks Too Much.* New York: Greenwillow Books, 1979.

———. *Living with a Parent Who Takes Drugs.* New York: Greenwillow Books, 1989.

Index

About the Author
Frannie Shuker-Haines is a free-lance writer currently living in Ann
Arbor, Michigan. She specializes in writing about parenting and child
rearing.

Acknowledgments and Photo Credits
Cover photo by Dick Smolinski.
Photograph on page 10: Wide World Photos. All other photos by Mary
Lauzon.

Design/Production: Blackbirch Graphics, Inc.